Executive Summary

Title: The Modern Catholic Just War Tradition

Author: Major Kevin Walsh, United States Marine Corps

Thesis: Among the competing interpretations of the Catholic Just War tradition, the one that is closest to the authentic teaching of the Church is the notion of a 'presumption against war', because it emphasizes the need for nations to exhaust every effort for peace, but ultimately the Church's approach asserts the overall obligation to promote justice. It is important for Catholics to understand the Church's teaching in order to embrace fully the Catholic Just War principles and make proper judgments regarding war and peace.

Discussion: Warfare in the modern era is especially destructive and has the potential to be worse in the years to come, which encouraged Catholic writers and thinkers to ask questions about how to apply the Just War tradition in the modern age. During the Twentieth Century the world endured two horribly destructive wars in Europe, which cost the lives of millions and arguably broke the backs of the European powers. The Pacific theater of war was brought to conclusion by the employment of two nuclear bombs on two separate Japanese cities and ushered in the nuclear age and the Cold War. While superpowers avoided a direct peer-on-peer war, the Cold War manifested itself in smaller conflicts throughout Asia and Central America and cultivated fear and suspicion among the world population brought about by the arms race. Once the Cold war was over, the proliferation of weapons and the problem of terrorism was prevalent. These conditions, which were exacerbated by high profile terrorist attacks, notably, the September 11, 2001 attacks on the twin towers, inspired a variety of different interpretations of the proper direction of the Just War tradition, because the circumstances revealed lethal types of warfare not present during the original formulation of the tradition. Three prominent points of view are at work in modern Catholic thought. They are not the result of the September 11 attacks, but the events of modern warfare provide a useful context for the necessity of developing a deeper understanding of the Just War tradition. One prevailing idea is the notion of pacifism[i]. Another can be referred to as the 'presumption against war'[ii], which is not quite pacifist, but has a powerful disposition against the use of violence. A third idea can be referred to as the 'presumption for justice'[iii], which does not relish the use of force; however, it asserts the concept that sometimes war is necessary in order to protect the common good. War is horrible and destructive and it is important to understand its moral context in order to develop clarity for decision making regarding war.

Conclusion: There are circumstances and times when good people and legitimate nations or communities may have to conduct war, but only after every effort for peace has been exhausted. The Catholic Church teaching does have a 'presumption against war', but justice is an enduring ideal.

DISCLAIMER

THE OPINIONS AND CONCLUSIONS EXPRESSED HEREIN ARE THOSE OF THE INDIVIDUAL STUDENT AUTHOR AND DO NOT NECESSARILY REPRESENT THE VIEWS OF EITHER THE MARINE CORPS COMMAND AND STAFF COLLEGE OR ANY OTHER GOVERNMENTAL AGENCY. REFERENCES TO THIS STUDY SHOULD INCLUDE THE FOREGOING STATEMENT.

QUOTATION FROM, ABSTRACTION FROM, OR REPRODUCTION OF ALL OR ANY PART OF THIS DOCUMENT IS PERMITTED PROVIDED PROPER ACKNOWLEDGEMENT IS MADE.

Table of Contents

Preface

I selected the topic of the Catholic Just War tradition because I think it is very important to understand the proper moral reasoning for war, due to the tragic and horrible consequences of violent conflict. I am Catholic and it was natural for me to begin my examination with the Church, but in my personal reading I became aware of a tension among Catholic thinkers between three Catholic views of war, which are discussed in this thesis. I was curious to understand the grinding edges of the debate and that is why I chose to look at the problem by contrasting the views. The more I studied each view, I saw the differences, but I was struck by strong similarities. Pacifism was the most drastically different of them, but it was nested in the Church's teaching. The 'presumption against war' and the 'presumption for justice' seem to agree on some very basic premises, but which aspects of the Just War tradition to emphasize. The different aspects on which each view focuses lead to a different interpretation of when the use of force is appropriate in practice. I think it is necessary to evaluate and question when it is appropriate to use force or go to war, because war is so destructive.

Dr Rebecca Johnson acted as my mentor during the process. She is very well versed in the topic. She helped me to formulate my ideas and she provided comprehensive feedback throughout the process. She provided sources for me to examine and offered useful suggestions regarding different perspectives regarding the topic. She was vigilant in holding me to a high standard of scholarship and writing. She was enthusiastic, supportive, and extremely professional. I thank her for agreeing to be my mentor and for all of her help.

The questions regarding the Catholic Just War tradition are relevant to me, personally. Since I am a Marine, I have participated in war and may be called to do so again. Since I am Catholic, I am called to act in a way that is just and consistent with the truth. It is important for me deepen my understanding of the Church's teaching regarding war in order to understand my role in Iraq and Afghanistan, but also to evaluate possible future conflicts in which I may be called to serve. It is significant for me to recognize and study the moral context from a practical and professional perspective. This study was an opportunity for me to explore aspects of my faith and deepen my professional understanding at the same time.

Introduction

The Catholic Just War tradition seems easy to understand on the surface, but among modern Catholic thinkers there are differing approaches to the meaning of the Just War tradition and how it applies to the modern world. While the idea that nations should be able to use force to defend themselves seems uncontroversial, some Catholic thinkers argue that the example of Jesus presents the notion that nonviolence is the only appropriate answer to any problems in the world.[iv] Aside from this pacifist notion, other Catholic theologians argue that there are circumstances that exist in which war can be justified, but those conditions are so stringent and the burden of proof is so severe, it is rarely possible in the real world to classify a violent conflict as morally justified[v]. At the other end of the spectrum, there are Catholic writers who assert the idea that war is not only justified at times, but morally obligatory[vi]. There are many sources from tradition and scripture for Catholics to derive God's will on these matters and among the most authoritative is the writings and pronouncements of the Popes. Pope John Paul II and Pope Benedict XVI have spoken at length about the need for peace, but neither has offered extensive clarification regarding the Just War doctrine. Their comments on peace imply their intentions regarding the Just War tradition. The contrast of the three distinct points of view and the writings of Pope John Paul II and Pope Benedict XVI raise questions regarding the Catholic Just War tradition, which perhaps has been taken for granted until the age of modern warfare. What is the appropriate understanding of Just War tradition from a Catholic point of view?

Warfare in the modern era is especially destructive and has the potential to be worse in the years to come, which encouraged Catholic writers and thinkers to ask questions about how the Just War tradition applies in the modern age. During the Twentieth Century the world endured two horribly destructive wars in Europe, which cost the lives of millions and arguably broke the backs of the European powers. The Pacific theater of war was brought to conclusion by the employment of two nuclear bombs on two separate Japanese cities and ushered in the nuclear age and the Cold War. The Cold War, while superpowers avoided a direct peer-on-peer war, was characterized by smaller conflicts throughout Asia and Central America, as well as the fear and suspicion brought about by the arms race. Once the Cold war was over, the proliferation of weapons and the problem of terrorism became prevalent. These conditions, which were exacerbated by high profile terrorist attacks, notably the September 11, 2001 attacks on the twin towers, inspired a variety of different interpretations of the proper direction of the Just War tradition. The three prominent points of view of pacifism, 'presumption against war', and 'presumption for justice' in modern Catholic thought emerged over time. War is horrible and destructive and it is important to understand its moral context in order to develop clarity for decision making regarding war.

The Catholic Church through the Just War tradition does emphasize the need for nations to exhaust every effort for peace and, therefore, it does appear to have a 'presumption against war', but the approach is more nuanced. Catholic Just War tradition acknowledges the terrible consequences of war and it also emphasizes the common good or justice, because its focus is the right of nations to defend themselves and protect what is morally good with an appropriate use of force.[vii] Catholic teaching states that leaders are obligated to protect their citizens.[viii] The Church teaches that leaders must also first work for peace. [ix] Working for peace is closer to the heart of the matter for the Church, due to the destructive nature of war, but Catholic teaching also acknowledges that there are times when leaders with good intentions may find themselves in circumstances in which force is the only way to protect their people[x]. The Church recognizes the decision regarding the use of force is a prudential matter [xi]within the purview of the state leader and a moral state leader will focus first on peace, but will use force in a responsible and proportional way if it is necessary[xii].

The Catholic Just War tradition and these ideas regarding its modern interpretations present a useful framework for coming to a proper understanding of the proper role for war in human society. It is necessary to consider the scriptural and traditional origins of the Catholic Church's teaching on the Just War, in particular passages from the New Testament and the writings of Saint Augustine and Saint Thomas Aquinas, in order to grasp each of the distinct modern interpretations. Once the background is established, a discussion of each of the different points of view regarding the Just War tradition will be more fruitful. It is important to consider the comments by Pope John Paul II and Pope Benedict XVI concerning war and peace in order to understand the mind of the Catholic Church regarding these issues. The entire discussion will facilitate an answer to the question of the proper understanding of the Just War tradition in the modern era.

Background

The scriptural underpinnings of the Just War tradition of the Church are solid, but not extensive. The New Testament, which is the most appropriate starting point for this discussion, does not contain extensive or explicit direction on war. The New Testament records that Jesus spoke at length regarding a great many moral issues, but he did not address war or the conduct of war directly. In developing the Just War tradition, the Catholic Church refers to certain passages of scripture as guides for the appropriate understanding of war and violence[xiii].

The primary witness of the New Testament regarding any matter is the words and example of Jesus. Jesus in His personal witness was very peaceful. He healed the sick and forgave sinners. He spoke of the love of God and He ultimately died on the cross, while offering no resistance. In fact, He directed Peter to 'put down your sword' [xiv]when Peter tried to prevent Jesus from being arrested. He chased the money changers out of the temple with a stick, but He did not injure anybody physically as far as the account goes[xv]. However, the incident with the money changers can be understood as an example of Jesus using force in a limited and proportional way to protect the common good of the temple. Absent an explicit teaching on war, the example of Jesus does not seem to lend itself to justifying war and, as a result, the early Church lived as pacifists[xvi].

The Catechism of the Catholic Church describes certain principles of self-defense and defense of the common good with scriptural references, which uphold an understanding of the Just War tradition. A person has a right to self-defense. This right is associated with one's obligation to love oneself, which was directed by Jesus, when He commanded His followers to "love your neighbor as yourself."[xvii] The catechism extends the meaning of this passage to those who are responsible for the safety of others and those with proper authority. It explains that those in proper authority have a right and an obligation to protect the people for whom they are responsible even with military force, due to the right of self-defense guaranteed by Christ's demand that a person loves himself and his neighbor.

The Catechism of the Catholic Church explains that the military profession is a morally good pursuit, because it is associated with defending the common good.[xviii] This notion, as discussed by St. Augustine, is supported by scripture. The notable references in the New Testament are the story of the Centurion with a sick servant. He asked Jesus to cure his servant and during the event he identified himself as a soldier. Jesus cured the soldier's servant and at no time rebuked him for being a soldier.[xix] John the Baptist was approached by soldiers, who asked him specifically what they must do to be saved and he told them, "Do not practice extortion, do not falsely accuse anyone, and be satisfied with your wages."[xx] John did not tell the soldiers to give up being soldiers or imply that the profession itself was morally wrong. These passages lend credence to the idea that the military profession is a noble one, because there are times when war is justified and at those times those who fight the wars are defending the common good[xxi].

St. Augustine, who was one of the Church Fathers, initially defined the Just War tradition in a rudimentary way in order to describe how Christian charity manifested itself, when faced with violent unprovoked aggression against a person or groups of innocent people.[xxii] St. Augustine expressed that war was devastating and terrible, but sometimes a good and just person or society may find themselves in circumstances in which they could not avoid war[xxiii]. St. Augustine indicated that if a good person were forced to participate in a war, that it would be best if it was a war for righteousness.[xxiv] St. Augustine made the argument regarding soldiers himself[xxv]. He emphasized the importance of peace and that it was essential for Christians to pursue peace and be committed to peace in all that they do. He understood that the true nature of Jesus and the life a Christian was ordered toward peace, but he acknowledged the world is broken as a result of original sin and consequently good people would find it necessary to defend themselves using force. While he understood that war was necessary in certain circumstances, St. Augustine, admonished Christians that they were not permitted to hate or seek vengeance[xxvi]. War was strictly a matter of a just cause carried out for the common good and not an act of blood lust. St. Augustine developed the Just War tradition as a way of explaining how Christians could follow the example of Jesus Christ in unconditional love and how that unconditional love expressed itself in a case of unprovoked aggression against peaceful people.

St. Augustine focused on two primary themes, order and right intention, in the development of his rudimentary notion of the Just War[xxvii]. He constructed his ideas amidst a violent time of turmoil in the Roman Empire[xxviii], which required a theological response. In his work, *The City of God*, he put forth the idea that humans lived in two 'cities', which were not physical, but metaphysical. The city of earth was the physical world that humans could see and recognize with their physical senses, which was corrupted and broken. The city of God was the Heavenly Kingdom, which was invisible but was a reality of perfection and utter good.[xxix] Human beings dwelled in the destruction and degradation of the city of earth and human nature itself was flawed. St. Augustine's theme of order applied to governments. Government provided some modicum of order, albeit imperfect, in the chaotic city of earth and threats to that order needed to be neutralized in order to restore the order or the imperfect peace. According to St. Augustine, war was not the ideal way to restore order, but it was justifiable, because the imperfect peace of government was preferable to complete chaos and lawlessness[xxx]. St. Augustine's second theme of 'right intention' described the intent of the person engaged in warfare. The person engaged in warfare or the government declaring war must do so with the intention of restoring the peace. The intent of the war must be to restore the imperfect order that existed prior to the conflict.[xxxi] These two themes made up the backbone of St. Augustine's rudimentary form of the Catholic Just War tradition.

St. Thomas Aquinas, a Doctor of the Catholic Church and widely regarded as one of the most brilliant theologians in history, further refined the Just War tradition in order to provide clarity. St. Thomas Aquinas, using his point and counter-point method, discussed the Just War in great detail, providing different perspectives, including the ideas of St. Augustine. St. Thomas Aquinas described certain criteria in order for a war to be considered justifiable. The first criteria is, "the authority of the sovereign by whose command the war is to be waged",[xxxii] or proper authority. The second is, "a just cause is required, namely that those who are attacked should be attacked because they deserve it on account of some fault"[xxxiii]. The third criterion is, "belligerents should have a right intention, so that they intend the advancement of good, or the avoidance of evil."[xxxiv] During his explanations of each point, St. Thomas Aquinas referred to St. Augustine and built on the reasoning of St. Augustine, as well as scripture. Similar to St. Augustine, St. Thomas Aquinas made clear that war in many ways cut against the core of what it meant to be a Christian, but it could be justified under these narrow conditions. St. Thomas Aquinas was able to further clarify the murky ideas surrounding the moral context of war.

The first of the Just War criteria, which St. Thomas Aquinas developed, was 'proper authority'. The idea of 'proper authority' is an extension of St. Augustine's idea that governments in a limited way preserve order. St. Augustine's view of the government is that it was necessary, because there would be total havoc if there was not a coercive force to keep human beings from exercising their worst instincts, but St. Thomas Aquinas' view was more positive.[xxxv] St. Thomas Aquinas believed that human beings were made by God and destined for God, but government was an expression of human community. He believed that, despite the fallen nature of humans, God's goodness could show through them with the help of His Grace. St. Thomas thought humans could demonstrate the ability to live relatively peacefully with one another in community[xxxvi]. Government was a reflection of that community and a sign of order. The leader of the government was justified in using force to defend the city, because the legitimate leader was a natural part of the government order[xxxvii]. The leader, as a representative of the government, has the 'proper authority' to conduct war if it is necessary to preserve the government.

The second criteria for St. Thomas Aquinas' Just War tradition was 'just cause'. Typically, 'just cause' was considered a government's defense of itself from attack or some wrong done to it. Bishop Fulton Sheen, a widely respected Catholic theologian, asserted the following regarding 'just cause',

> 'Now, wars are of two kinds, defensive and offensive. A defensive war is just in its cause if it is waged to defend an essential and fundamental right unjustly denied. An offensive war is just in its action if it is the only means for preserving an essential and fundamental right or justice unjustly denied.'[xxxviii]

St. Thomas Aquinas' formulation of the 'just cause' is the second criteria of his Just War tradition.

The third criterion of the Just War tradition, postulated by St. Thomas Aquinas, was 'right intention'. This criterion is an extension of St. Augustine's idea that a person or a leader engaged in war always must seek the good. The intention must be always the good not only of the one's government or nation, but the good of the enemy as well. The leader or individual must never succumb to revenge or desire for domination, but must seek to restore peace at all times[xxxix].

St. Augustine and St. Thomas Aquinas formulated much of the underpinning of Catholic thought regarding the Just War tradition and their respective updates demonstrate the incremental evolution of the tradition. St. Augustine developed a rudimentary version of the tradition in response to the violent and maelstrom in the Roman Empire at the time[xl]. St. Thomas Aquinas upgraded and fleshed out the tradition, during the calmer Medieval Era[xli]. St. Augustine and St.

Thomas Aquinas developed the basis for the Catholic Just War tradition and inaugurated a process in which the tradition has been debated continually by Catholic thinkers.

The Catholic Church's most authoritative teaching on the Just War tradition is found in the Catechism of the Catholic Church; and it is necessary to begin any discussion of the Catholic Just War tradition with the Catechism. The Catechism, referred to earlier regarding self-defense, formally describes the circumstances, that justify resorting to war. The Catechism defines the circumstances for a Just War as follows:

> All citizens and all governments are obliged to work for the avoidance of war. However, 'as long as the danger of war persists and there is no international authority with the necessary competence and power, governments cannot be denied the right of lawful self-defense, once all peace efforts have failed.'[xlii]
>
> The strict conditions for legitimate defense by military force require rigorous consideration. The gravity of such a decision makes it subject to rigorous conditions of moral legitimacy. At one and the same time:
>
> - the damage inflicted by the aggressor on the nation or community of nations must be lasting, grave, and certain;
>
> - all other means of putting an end to it must have been shown to be impractical or ineffective;
>
> - there must be serious prospects of success;
>
> - the use of arms must not produce evils and disorders graver than the evil to be eliminated. The power of modem means of destruction weighs very heavily in evaluating this condition.

These are the traditional elements enumerated in what is called the "just war" doctrine. The evaluation of these conditions for moral legitimacy belongs to the prudential judgment of those who have responsibility for the common good[xliii]

The elements of scripture, St. Thomas Aquinas and St. Augustine are present in the Catechism's discussion of the Just War tradition. All of the elements are fused together in a way that provides a theoretical and moral background for a discussion of the differing interpretations of the Just War tradition in the modern era. The pacifist logic reflects a view which emphasizes the ideas reflected in the first sentence of the above quote. Similarly, the 'presumption against war' view implies reasoning present in portions of the above quote, which refer to war as a last resort and the 'strict conditions for legitimate defense'. The ideas of the 'presumption for justice' view express notions articulated by the Catechism in the portions of the above quote concerning the 'moral legitimacy belongs to the prudential judgment of those who have responsibility for the common good'. The elements of scripture, St. Thomas Aquinas' ideas, and St. Augustine's formulations abound in the Catechism's discussion of the Just War tradition.

The Pacifist View

The pacifist view of the Just War tradition, as expressed by Fr. John Dear, is that the tradition should be jettisoned for a greater commitment to nonviolence[xliv]. Given the history of the Just War tradition, this pacifist vision may seem unorthodox, but there is merit to reasoning. The reasoning is that Jesus is the model and the example all Christians are intended to follow and Jesus was nonviolent.[xlv] While that is the crux of the argument, it goes deeper than that and explains that God is peace and is nonviolent. Anything violent is outside of God or separates the person from God. Jesus entered into history to demonstrate victory over evil and violence and human beings should trust His way. When human beings resort to violence even in self-defense, they fail to trust Jesus and they cooperate with the warlike and evil forces of the world. Fr. Dear describes the 'world' as being predicated on violence and destruction.[xlvi] Jesus came to overcome the world by offering an example and the power of peace. Similar to Fr. John Dear, Dorothy Day, founder of the Catholic Worker movement and committed Catholic pacifist referred to scripture to argue on behalf of non-violence,

> Christians when they are seeking to defend their faith by arms, by force and violence, are like those who said to our Lord, 'Come down from the Cross. If you are the Son of God, save Yourself.'
>
> But Christ did not come down from the Cross. He drank to the last drop the agony of His suffering and was not part of the agony, the hopelessness, the unbelief of His own disciples?
>
> Christ is being crucified today, every day. Shall we ask Him with the unbelieving world to come down from the cross? Or shall we joyfully, as His brothers, 'Complete the sufferings of Christ'?[xlvii]

Fr. Dear insists that the way to follow Jesus is to be nonviolent, pray for nonviolence, protest violence, and love your neighbors and your enemies.

Fr. Dear argues that the Just War tradition was never compatible with Christianity and it was an accommodation made because the path of nonviolence was too challenging.[xlviii] Fr. Dear suggests that the Church should abandon the Just War tradition and return to the model of the early Church, prior to the development of the tradition. He claims the early Church experienced persecutions and was nonviolent, but later the Church developed the Just War tradition in a compromise fashion rather than promote the difficult teaching of nonviolence.[xlix] Fr. Dear urges the Church to dispense with Just War reasoning and accept an entirely nonviolent approach, which would be a full embrace of the Gospel message and a more profound witness to God.

Drew Christiansen, SJ, editor of the Jesuit magazine *America*, makes the point that Pope John Paul II's role in the fall of communism was as a successful non-violent response to evil in the world[l]. The Catholic pacifists, such as Fr. Dear and Dorothy Day, urge patience as part of the non-violent response to evil in the world. An understandable concern regarding the pacifist movement is how does it confront evil? The pacifist approach can seem to be confined to protests such as the Catholic Worker Movement conducted or the demonstrations in which Fr. John Dear participated. Drew Christiansen points to an example of pacifism, which operated on a much larger scale. He argues that Pope John Paul II through his support of the Solidarity Movement in Poland helped bring about the fall of communism in Poland in a non-violent way[li]. The example may have flaws, but the larger point is that there are non-violent ways to bring about change by leveraging the power of culture and community at a national level, which can be effective in putting pressure on dictators and tyrants. He makes the point further that the Catholic Bishops have acknowledged the usefulness of pacifism, not merely as an individual vocation, but as a course of action for the Catholic community[lii]. Pope John Paul II's support for the resistance to communism is arguably an example of a successful non-violent strategy to combat a form of evil or injustice.

The pacifist point of view is a compelling Catholic point of view, because of its inherent purity and idealism. It claims to take the Catholic Christian message at face value. They take seriously the notion that Jesus came into the world to radically change or reform the way humans viewed the world. Due to the "fall" in the Garden of Eden, the 'world' operates under a dimmed or broken understanding of justice and truth. The 'world's' view is that the powerful establish what is right and the strong survive. Jesus came in humility and poverty to demonstrate and to proclaim that justice is based on truth and love rather than power. These are simplified paraphrases of the Catholic pacifist views, but essentially they express the basis for their understanding of non-violence. Jesus conquered sin and death by giving Himself up on the cross. He refused to cooperate with the paradigm that 'might makes right' by using His power to destroy His enemies through physical force. Instead, Jesus vanquished His true enemy; death, with love and forgiveness. The idea that Catholics are called to follow the example of Jesus and rely on love instead of physical violence in order to bring about justice and true peace is a pacifist notion which resonates deeply within the Catholic self-understanding. The Church does realize that the call of Christ is one of radical transformation. The Church does comprehend that God's ways are not the ways of humanity and God's solutions to the problems of the world require faith. Catholics realize they are called to bear witness to nobler humanity defined and exemplified by Christ. The pacifist point of view is attractive to the Catholic mind due to its pure and idealistic commitment to the example of Jesus.

Flaws in the pacifist point of view are associated with its unwillingness to address self-defense. While Jesus chose not to defend Himself, when it came time to be crucified, it is not clear that Jesus intended for everyone to endure oppressive evil with no resistance at all. It is not the Catholic understanding that a person should sit and pray, while an intruder kills his wife and children. The person in that case has the right to use force, if necessary, to stop the intruder from harming his family. The person in this case would not be cooperating with evil as much as protecting justice. This is not the same as the Just War, but the principle is similar. The principle is that evil should not be allowed to go unchecked or without resistance in this world. This principle is not adequately addressed in the Pacifist point of view. Using force as a last resort in order to protect the innocent or the helpless does not violate love. It protects the good and preserves the common good. The pacifist point of view tends to seem utopian in its vision. It lends itself to an overly simplistic interpretation, which makes it seem unrealistic. Its message can seem to postulate that, if enough people refused to participate in violence, those who use violence would be pressured to cease and the world would be more peaceful. The Pacifist message is deeper than that, but without seriously addressing the legitimacy of self-defense, it can seem impractical, which is the primary flaw in the point of view.

The Pacifist point of view, expressed by Fr. John Dear and others, claims that the Just War tradition does not fit with the true teachings of Jesus, because Jesus was non-violent himself. They understand the example of Jesus to be directly contrary to the notion of a justified use of violence[liii]. Pacifists assert that the Just War tradition was an accommodation[liv] made as a compromise position for the Catholic Church. The example of Pope John Paul II's non-violent strategy against communism during the 1970s and 1980s provides a new approach for pacifism on a larger level. The pacifist point of view makes a compelling case that the example of Jesus Christ included a robust response to evil, but was completely non-violent.

Presumption Against War

Another modern view of the Catholic Just War tradition can be referred to as the 'presumption against war' and it states that war theoretically can be justifiable under specific terms though it almost never is due to a presumption against war. One of the proponents of this idea is Paul J. Griffiths, who is a professor of Catholic studies at Duke University, and he argues a number of points, including that there is a strict burden of proof required to justify war, war must be declared with proper authority, and it always must be a last resort[lv]. These points can be found in the Catechism's discussion of the Just War tradition, as well and Griffith's argues that these points make it very difficult to justify war in the modern world. According to Griffith it is possible that a certain war may be just, but it is almost impossible for an individual to make that judgment[lvi], because an individual would not be privy to the information necessary to make the judgment. This view is not a pacifist view, like the views of Fr. John Dear, because it does acknowledge the theoretical, theological, and philosophical reasons which can be used to justify the use of force; however, the view in practice severely restricts the ability to justify circumstances for war in the real world. The presumption against war is so rigid that rarely can war be justified in the world according to this view.

The 'presumption against war' point of view starts with the portion of the Catechism, which states, "All citizens and all governments are obliged to work for the avoidance of war."[lvii] It also states, "The strict conditions for legitimate defense by military force require rigorous consideration. The gravity of such a decision makes it subject to rigorous conditions of moral legitimacy."[lviii] This point of view understands these passages in the Catechism of the Catholic Church as reflecting accurately the teachings of scripture as well as the tradition handed down in Church teaching from St. Augustine and St. Thomas Aquinas. The view is that war is heinous and destructive, but more importantly it is a departure from Jesus Himself, who is the Prince of Peace. War is never a good option, but in tradition there are times when it may be necessary. However, there are strict criteria for the times when war is justified and it is very difficult to meet that standard, because the onus is on humanity to work for peace. The 'presumption against war' interprets these aspects of the Catholic Just War tradition to indicate that war is not a last resort merely, but that war should be resisted with exhaustive effort.

One of the aspects of this interpretation of the Just War tradition, which makes it difficult to justify the use of force, is the burden of proof. Griffiths argues that the burden of proof to go to war is similar to that used to convict a person of murder[lix]. In a sense, a nation, when it considers going to war, is considering sentencing some members of another nation to death and, therefore, according to the argument they must prove beyond a reasonable doubt that the other nation is guilty of transgressions, which merit war. Griffiths argues from the point of view of Catholic citizens of a nation; which intends to go to war, and not necessarily from the perspective of a leader of the nation; however, the principles apply for leaders as well. He argues that there must be a presumption of innocence and that the nation, which intends to go to war, must prove the guilt of the object of the war[lx]. The presumption of innocence is a stringent standard for the average citizen as well as for the leader of a nation.

According to this view, the leader must have and must present to the citizens of the nation irrefutable proof beyond a reasonable doubt that the cause for war is justifiable. While the leader of a nation is typically understood to be the 'proper authority', the citizens ought to consent to the government and the citizens, including Catholics, will execute any given war and it is relevant for them to give consent or not. George Weigel, who represents the 'presumption of justice' view to be discussed later, agrees that there is a burden of proof requirement, but he does not take it as far as Griffiths[lxi]. Griffith acknowledges that it is very difficult for a nation to meet such a stringent burden of proof to its citizens and to the world at large. This makes it very difficult for Catholic citizens to support any war in which their nation may participate[lxii]. It also makes it very difficult for leaders of a nation to discern the justification for war.

Griffiths also acknowledges that this is a very high standard in the modern era with unique threats and a complex information environment[lxiii]. The burden of proof aspect of this point of view is very difficult to meet circumstances involving two sovereign states, but it becomes especially complicated when non-state actors are involved. Griffiths asserts the average Catholic citizen cannot trust the information he/she receives from the media or the government and, therefore, is never in a position to accurately discern whether a specific war is justified or not. He referred specifically to US Catholics and claimed that the US government has lied before regarding reasons for war and the US media is biased and unreliable as well and that makes it almost impossible for US Catholics to support any war in which the US may participate.[lxiv] The leader may have access to more information, but the burden of proof standard is still a difficult one to meet, when faced with responding to terrorist organizations and other non-state actors.

The connections non-state actors have to an actual state are often difficult to define and terrorist organizations tend to be decentralized, which makes targeting and justifying war or military action against them very difficult especially when applying the burden of proof standard. The burden of proof standard is one aspect of the 'presumption against war' view, which makes it almost impossible to justify any war.

This rigid interpretation of the burden of proof criteria is inflexible to the point of being inoperable. It is commendable to prevent war at all costs and it to avoid war should be the goal of any nation, but to make it conditional upon irrefutable proof is unrealistic and could prevent a nation from taking military action in a timely manner. In matters of war, time can be a factor because the aggressor nation may be able to mobilize if the just nation does not act quickly. The just nation may lose valuable time for its own mobilization against an aggressor nation, while trying to meet the extreme burden of proof. The justified nation may never be able to meet the stringent burden of proof criteria, which the 'presumption against war view' advocates, despite actually being justified. The possible consequences would be an aggressor nation or non-state actor causing destruction with no resistance. No nation should rush to war without a clear understanding of the moral dimensions of the situation. Catholic citizens should ask questions regarding the moral reasoning behind any given conflict. Catholic citizens also should hold their representatives accountable for their integrity (at least in the United States), so they can feel more confident about trusting them in matters of war and peace, but still the citizens should not do so blindly. If a nation has conducted due diligence in attempting to find solutions other than war, it and its Catholic citizenry should not be hamstrung by an overly rigid interpretation of the burden of proof criteria. The burden of proof criteria should not be inflexible to the point of being inoperable.

Another aspect of the 'presumption against war' is the standard of proper authority and the interpretation of how proper authority should be defined. Historically, proper authority was understood to mean the sovereign leader of a nation or community. It was discussed by St. Augustine and St. Thomas Aquinas in order to emphasize that individual citizens were not authorized to declare war or conduct war on their own or by their own authority.[lxv] The idea was that the authority of a sovereign leader was given to that leader ultimately by God, similar to the way in which Jesus acknowledged Pilate's authority.[lxvi] Bishop Fulton Sheen, during a discussion of right intention and the common good, indirectly implied the usefulness of an organization such as the UN, "The common good here means not exclusively the common good of the individual nation but the common good of the world, because today no nation is hermetically sealed but rather its order and prosperity is bound up inseparably with other nations."[lxvii] However, the Catechism of the Catholic Church states, "as long as the danger of war persists and there is no international authority with the necessary competence and power, governments cannot be denied the right of lawful self-defense, once all peace efforts have failed."[lxviii] Proponents of the 'presumption against war' argue that in the modern world the understanding of proper authority can be broadened or expanded to include the United Nations (UN). Prior to the establishment of the UN (or the League of Nations before it), countries did not have a forum within which they could discuss their differences and air their grievances in civilized way[lxix]. The result of this situation was that the sovereign leaders dealt with each other directly and unilaterally with no outside objective arbiter. According to the 'presumption against war' proponents, it was reasonable for the leader of a nation to be the final proper authority under the Just War tradition in these circumstances, but now that nations have an arena to discuss issues and the ability to make use of objective third parties in the UN, it is appropriate for the UN to fill that role[lxx]. The idea is not that the UN would certify formally all conflicts in the world, but that nations would first discuss their problems and justifications in the UN and gain input from other nations. If the UN is not considered the proper authority, it must be understood at least that nations should not act unilaterally in declaring or conducting wars. Griffiths is not the only Catholic voice to emphasize the need for a coalition. Russell Shaw, a catholic author who writes on issues concerning Catholics, in an interview regarding the US decision to go to war in Iraq in 2003 stated,

> "...the United States is hardly the only country that will be impacted by what does or doesn't happen in Iraq, so it is unilateralism to say the only prudential judgment that counts rests with the civil authorities of the United States. Many nations have interests at stake here and have a right to be involved in the decision."[lxxi]

Proponents of the 'presumption against war' point of view perceive the UN as one more step or another obstacle on the path to war, which will enable leaders of good will more time and more opportunities to find some other solution rather than war.

The understanding of proper authority cannot be separated from a nation's leader. The forum of the UN is a useful resource, but can never mitigate the responsibility of the leader. The 'presumption against war' point of view recognizes important aspects of proper authority and makes reasonable arguments against one nation acting unilaterally in the decision to engage in war, but a nation should reserve the right to do so if it deems necessary. The beauty of the UN is that it does provide a forum for nations, which want to preserve peace and at the same time protect their interests, to find solutions to their problems other than conflict. The UN can be a place where peace loving nations can come together to condemn aggression and violence and form coalitions to resist destructive forces together. The UN is a conduit in which nations can collaborate in order to discover ways to deal with violent non-state actors. These things are good and accentuate the point that nations should not act unilaterally. While that is true, there is no guarantee that justice will be accomplished at the UN. There is no assurance that a coalition will form behind what is right. Justice is not achieved by consensus. Consensus may align against justice or a justified nation. Therefore, the leader of the nation is the proper authority and makes the decision to go to war according to the specific governmental practices of his/her nation. It is desirable and wise for a nation to consult it neighbors through the UN and to gain a coalition, if war is necessary. The onus and responsibility of proper authority must remain with the leader of a given nation.

Another aspect of the Catholic Just War tradition, on which the proponents of the 'presumption against war' point of view focus, is the requirement that war be a last resort. This aspect is simple to understand, but is less simple in practice. The Catechism of the Catholic Church is clear that war is only justified, "once all peace efforts have failed."[lxxii] The circumstances under which all peace efforts have failed seems subjective. Since it is subjective, it is connected to proper authority and to the Church's assertion that these decisions, "…belongs to the prudential judgment of those who have responsibility for the common good."[lxxiii] The emphasis for proponents of the 'presumption against war' interpretation is that leaders and individual citizens should be so committed to peace that they will leave no stone unturned in order to avoid war. Bishop Fulton Sheen articulated the idea that war must be a last resort as well, "It is, of course, here presumed that the war is the last resort in the preservation of justice; that <every> other peaceful means of righting the wrong must have been tried…"[lxxiv] This includes the use of diplomacy, if necessary, arbitrated or informed by the UN or a third party of some kind, with a true spirit of negotiation.

Prior to declaring war or undertaking military action, a nation must be willing to negotiate through diplomacy and make some concessions in order to avoid war. When nations are separated by long histories of violence often aggravated by recent offenses, the proponents of the 'presumption against war' view recommend forgiveness.[lxxv] Forgiveness may seem like a notion that has no place in international affairs, but proponents argue that it is necessary to enable peace negotiations to go further and to avoid the occasion of war as well as the continued cycle of war perpetuated by war itself. The idea of war as a last resort, as interpreted by those who are proponents of the 'presumption against war', includes a radical willingness to avoid war and to pursue every effort for peace.

The 'presumption against war' point of view begins with an understanding that war is destructive and terrible and should be avoided at almost any cost to the point in which it is very difficult in a practical sense to identify any justifiable conflict according to its interpretation. The aspects of the Just War tradition, which this viewpoint emphasizes, are derived from the tradition reflected in the Catechism of the Catholic Church. The burden of proof, proper authority, and the idea that war should be a last resort are all things expressed in the Catechism of the Catholic Church or can be implied, when reading it. The standards by which these ideas are understood are matters subject to interpretations. The proponents of this view maintain a very high threshold for the justification of the use of military force, because they believe the consequences of war are so horrendous.

The 'presumption against war' point of view represents a radical perspective in its own right. It is not a middle of the road between pacifism and 'presumption for justice'. It has pacifist roots, but acknowledges circumstances in which war would be justified. It leans heavily toward finding ways other than war to solve problems. It reflects the serious moral and intellectual rigor necessary to justify war, according to the Catholic interpretation of the Just War tradition. It demonstrates the realism of understanding that war is a part of this fallen world and sometimes the use of force is justified, but also the idealistic view that peace is what is best and peace can be achieved. Peace can be achieved many times, if nations and people are not so eager to use force. It may be too rigid in its understanding of burden of proof and have a disordered understanding of the role of the UN, but ultimately it is committed to peace. The 'presumption against war' is extreme in its dedication to peace, but intellectually does not dismiss the logic of St. Augustine, St. Thomas Aquinas, and the Catechism of the Catholic Church that war is justified in certain circumstances no matter how terrible it is.

The radical nature of the 'presumption against war' view's devotion to peace is quintessentially Catholic. Similar to the pacifist view, the 'presumption against war' understands Catholics believe they are called to a radical witness in this world. Part of that witness is dedication to peace. Catholics believe they are called to be 'peacemakers' and it requires hard work, patience, and sacrifice. The pursuit of peace is connected to the cross and forgiveness.

Therefore, a realist understanding of the use of force in international affairs is not compatible with the Church's teachings or the witness to Jesus. The admission of the justification for war under specific conditions is not a compromise by the Church to the realpolitik, but is an acknowledgement of the necessity for nations to maintain the common good within the larger pursuit of peace. In fact, the 'presumption against war' view understands that the goal of war, if it is unavoidable, is to restore peace. The 'presumption against war' view is radically Catholic, because it reflects the exhaustive pursuit of peace, but acknowledges that sometimes war is necessary to restore the order and harmony necessary for peace to flourish.

Presumption for Justice

A third general point of view regarding the Catholic Just War tradition is termed for the purpose of this discussion the 'presumption for justice', which justifies the use of force in order to maintain order and justice for the common good despite the horrible consequences of war. George Weigel, a Catholic America writer/philosopher/conservative political commentator, is a strong proponent of this point of view. He has written extensively regarding the Catholic Just War tradition and suggests a new understanding of the tradition must be constructed in order to enable it to apply to the new modern threats such as terrorism and non-state actors[lxxvi]. Weigel applies the Catholic Just War tradition by focusing on the common good, the moral obligation to defend justice, clarification of the role of a nation at war versus an individual person's participation in violence, and clarification of the difference between the justification of war and the moral conduct of war[lxxvii]. Emphasis on these points tends to shape a discussion in a different direction. The conversation, while it acknowledges how terrible war is, does not dwell as much on that aspect as on how important it is to maintain the common good or justice. As a result, the threshold for the moral justification for war is less rigid. Weigel would argue it is more practical, but in keeping with Gospel[lxxviii]. The 'presumption for justice' is expressed as the idea that a state of injustice (or where the common good is endangered) is worse than a state of war. According to this thinking, the purpose for any war should be the restoration of justice and the common good[lxxix]. The 'presumption for justice' emphasizes that it is more important to preserve or protect justice than it is to avoid war.

George Weigel argues in favor of 'presumption for justice' or the common good rather than a 'presumption against war'. He states that in the Catholic Just War tradition there historically was no presumption against violence. Instead, he states that there the common good was emphasized.[lxxx] Weigel refers to the fact that St. Thomas Aquinas' discussion of the Just War tradition was located within the context of his discussion regarding the virtue of Charity in order to demonstrate that the presumption regarding war emphasizes the need to maintain the good of the other rather than on a default position against violence. James Turner Johnson, who is Professor of Religion at Rutgers University, makes a similar point regarding St. Thomas Aquinas' logic regarding just cause, "Within the logic of Aquinas' just war theory, defense of the common good—protecting just order and therefore peace—is the central rationale for just war as a whole."[lxxxi] He refers to the scripture passage in which Jesus directs His followers to 'love your neighbor as yourself'[lxxxii] as further evidence that the initial presumption must be for the restoration of maintenance of justice and the common good rather than the avoidance of war. The Catechism of the Catholic Church, in a section concerning individual self-defense and not the section concerning war, states,

> Legitimate defense can be not only a right but a grave duty for someone responsible for another's life. Preserving the common good requires rendering the unjust aggressor unable to inflict harm. To this end, those holding legitimate authority have the right to

repel by armed force aggressors against the civil community entrusted to their charge.[lxxxiii]

It appears that Weigel and those who presume for justice rather than against war place greater weight on this aspect of Catholic teaching than on the admonishments regarding the exhaustion of all peace efforts. The 'presumption for justice' in the pursuit of the common good does not dismiss the obligation to make every effort for peace, but the efforts for peace must serve to maintain the justice. The 'presumption for justice' is not an enthusiasm for war, but it places greater weight on the preservation of the common good than on the terrible destructiveness of war.

Another aspect of this understanding of the Just War tradition is the notion that there is a moral obligation to use force if it is necessary to preserve justice[lxxxiv]. The above passage from the Catechism of the Catholic Church applies to this aspect the 'preservation of justice'. Weigel makes the point that it is a moral duty for leaders to employ force, if necessary, in order to defend their citizens from threats to their common good and justice[lxxxv]. James Turner Johnson reaffirms this point as well, "Insofar as the need for defense provides just cause for public use of the sword, it comes from the responsibility of government to protect order, justice, and peace, not simply from the right to respond to an attacker in kind."[lxxxvi] This appears to be a significant departure from the 'presumption against war' idea that war is an absolute last resort, which is entered into begrudgingly by leaders of good will. However, the argument is essentially, in circumstances which would suit the 'presumption against war' criteria for conducting a war, it is a moral obligation at that time not merely a legitimate option. The argument further assumes, in circumstances in which the maintenance of justice demanded war, that the nation would enter the war begrudgingly. It is the definition of the threshold for war, which is different between the two approaches (the pacifist approach is utterly different), not the notion that war is terrible or the idea that it is sometimes necessary. The threshold for those who make the 'presumption for justice' is less restrictive than those who 'presume against war', but Weigel would argue it is more practical and still consistent with the Gospel; in fact, it is the fulfillment of the obligation to love one's neighbor.

Weigel disagrees with the notion that the UN is a valid 'proper authority'. He acknowledges that proper authority is necessary, but argues that the national leader is a valid proper authority. James Turner Johnson makes a similar argument, when he describes current attitudes which undermine the idea of the legitimacy of the state. These attitudes give way to the idea that third party arbiters are necessary to decide whether a conflict is justified. Johnson discussed, in a written article, the modern notion of the state in relation to the UN or organizations like it,

> "recent Catholic thought on war often treats the state as a locus of injustice and the goals
> of particular states as inherently at odds with the achievement of common human goals,
> while an internationalism defined in terms of the United Nations system is proposed as
> the best means to those common goals."[lxxxvii]

Johnson contrasts this idea with the Classical idea that the sovereign was the protector of the common good or justice. [lxxxviii]The Catechism of the Catholic Church appears to support this perspective, "These are the traditional elements enumerated in what is called the "just war" doctrine. The evaluation of these conditions for moral legitimacy belongs to the prudential judgment of those who have responsibility for the common good."[lxxxix] Weigel's objection to the UN as the 'proper authority' focuses on the idea that the UN does not necessarily have moral credibility and does not reflect the values of the Catholic Church or any given nation. The UN and the Catholic Church are consistently at odds regarding matters such as abortion and birth control[xc], among other things which, while not directly relevant to the just war tradition, demonstrates significant divergence of values between them. Because of issues like these, Weigel and proponents of the 'presumption for justice' view argue it is more appropriate for the leader of a certain nation, who knows and reflects the value of his/her nation to make the decision for or against war rather than the UN or a coalition of nations.

The 'presumption for justice' view's criticism of the UN as proper authority is misplaced. The argument from the 'presumption against war' view is not that the UN would become the proper authority, but that nations should not go to war unilaterally. The point, made by Johnson, that nations are viewed as cauldrons of injustice incapable of making right decisions is valid, but it does not negate the good that can come from the emphasizing the UN as a forum for collaboration and arbitration. The idea that there are horrible actors who have influence in the UN and that the UN is at odds with the Catholic Church on a wide variety of issues is true, but that does not negate the utility of the UN. The UN is imperfect and it can be argued it is ineffective at times. There have been wars and conflicts around the world, since the UN was established, but there was no World War III. While the UN may not be the sole reason the world was able to avoid another kinetic world war, it was a factor. As discussed earlier, the UN can never replace a leader of a nation as proper authority, but the UN can provide a useful venue for nations to air their grievances and avoid war. The 'presumption for justice' view's criticism of the UN as a proper authority is misguided.

Weigel argues the 'presumption against war' tends to confuse the requirements and standards for an individual and the role and purpose of a leader representing a nation and that confusion leads to an improper idea of when force can morally be applied. He argues that there is a difference between a use of force for private ends and the use of force by a sovereign authority for purpose of preserving the common good[xci]. The use of force for private ends is limited and restricted and is described predominantly by self-defense. The principles of moral self-defense are applied at the national level, but the burdens of justification are more vague, because the responsibility of the leader of a nation to the people of the nation are more sweeping than that of the individual towards his neighbor. Weigel believes the responsibilities and roles regarding justice are greater for a nation than for an individual, and so, the necessity to use force may be more wide-ranging and he asserts that understanding the different requirements between the individual and the nation is key to recognizing the 'presumption for justice'[xcii].

The 'presumption for justice' view regarding the difference between a nation going to war and an individual involved in violence is in reference to the burden of proof criteria discussed earlier. The 'presumption for justice' view of the burden of proof for a nation to justify war is that the burden is not as severe as it would be for an individual to be convicted of murder. The argument was discussed earlier and it is that nations should not be held to such a stringent burden of proof, because it will hamstring the nation's ability to protect its people and preserve the common good. The notion of a burden of proof is correct but it is imprudent to insist the burden be so stringent.

Another aspect of confusion Weigel identifies is the confusion between the justification for war and the moral conduct of war. He claims that some Catholic theologians assign atrocities and human rights violations to all participants in war, especially modern war. Human rights violations and atrocities are perversions which sometimes occur during war, which make it even more terrible; however, when a nation has just cause to go to war, that nation will not necessarily engage in war in an immoral way[xciii]. Weigel asserts immoral conduct during a certain war does not negate the just purpose of that war. James Turner Johnson makes a similar point, "The morality of modern war, as of all war, depends on the moral choices of those who fight it. It is not the choice to fight that is inherently wrong, as the "presumption against war" argument has it; it is the choice to fight for immoral reasons and/or by immoral means."[xciv] Nations do not have a right to engage in atrocities ever, but in certain circumstances they do have the right to use war or force to defend their sovereignty or justice[xcv]. The Catechism of the Catholic Church affirms the idea that a just cause does not give a nation the right to commit human rights violations.[xcvi] Weigel believes the understandable repulsion towards the atrocities of war confuse the issue and lead some to believe that there must be a 'presumption against war' which is so rigid that it restricts the ability to preserve justice.[xcvii]

Weigel views the "presumption against war" point of view as functional pacifism, because it interprets the Just War tradition so rigidly that it is virtually impossible for a conflict to meet the requirements, which he claims does not fulfill the common good.[xcviii] James Turner Johnson makes the claim that in recent history Catholic thought has turned towards the notion that no modern wars may meet the criteria for a just war, due to the lethality of modern weapons and the viciousness of modern tactics and strategy.[xcix] According to that understanding, there is a de facto presumption against modern war as a rule, which could be viewed as functional pacifism. Weigel and the proponents of the presumption for justice view assert that the 'presumption against war' view translates into functional pacifism and fails to see the need to act with force on behalf of justice at certain times.

The notion of the 'presumption for justice', as opposed to the 'presumption against war', is based on many of the same notions, but with a different emphasis. George Weigel advocates for this point of view by describing an emphasis on preserving the common good, the obligation to use force in order to maintain justice, the confusion of the private use of forces and the public use of force, and the confusion of the moral conduct of war rather than the moral causes to participate in war. The 'presumption for justice' is the idea that Just War tradition has held that, as terrible as war is, a lack of justice is worse. Where there is an absence of war and an absence of justice there is no peace.

The 'presumption for justice' view appeals to the human sense that human beings should fight for what is right. It is a very natural and good reaction to unfairness and injustice in the world. Most people, including Catholics, enjoy the prospect of a bad actor being defeated or punished through the use of force by a good actor. Many are impatient with hesitation in response to injustice in the world. Many Catholics want to solve problems in this world in a bold manner even if that includes the use of force. This is not necessarily a bellicose attitude, but it reflects the inherent desire for fairness and justice contained within the human heart. The 'presumption for justice' reflects this attitude and presents it with a solid moral and traditional Catholic foundation. It is not careless, but it does fail to emphasize the 'last resort 'criteria of the Just War tradition enough. The 'presumption for justice' view subtly emphasizes action or force over the need to pursue peace in an exhaustive manner. It does not reflect a cavalier attitude or a 'rush to war' mentality, but it fails to embrace the spirit of the 'last resort' criteria for the Just War tradition adequately. It claims the 'presumption against war' view is a modern construct and it equates to 'functional pacifism', but it overlooks the spirit of the Church's teaching on the Just War. The 'presumption for justice' view acknowledges the importance of peace and, in fact, draws the conclusion that peace is so important at times war is necessary to preserve or restore it. The 'presumption against war' view actually would agree on this point, but the difference between the two perspectives is the emphasis placed on peace prior to a conflict. The 'presumption of war' view fails to properly appreciate the value of nations finding a peaceful solution to a problem, even a problem as horrible as an act of violent aggression by a nation against another or a wonton act of violence by a non-state actor. The spirit of the Catholic teaching on the Just War emphasizes peace to a greater degree than the 'presumption for justice' view. The Catholic view holds out the hope for peace even in situations of extreme violence when the prospects for peace seem dim. The 'presumption for justice' view appeals to the human sense of right and wrong and the human desire to act decisively in the face of injustice, but it does not capture entirely the Catholic Church's resolute commitment to peace.

Pope John Paul II and Pope Benedict XVI

The different perspectives on the Catholic Just War tradition represent interesting debates regarding the application of the Just War tradition on the future; however, the most authoritative voice regarding any aspect of Catholic teaching is the Supreme Pontiff. Pope John Paul II and Pope Benedict XVI have made several statements regarding peace and war since 1978. A good source to find the perspectives of Pope Benedict XVI and Pope John Paul II regarding war and peace are their respective messages for the annual World Day of Peace. The messages promote peace, but they discuss war, as well, and they shed light on each of the pontiff's understanding of the Christian view of war. Pope John Paul II and Pope Benedict XVI take seriously the call for Christians to work for peace and they emphasize the necessity of justice[c]. Neither Pope John Paul II nor Pope Benedict XVI have clarified or added emphasis to the Just War tradition in their writings or speeches, but both discuss war and emphasize the need for peace[ci]. While the pontiffs are not pacifist, they urge the world to embrace peace and they call attention to the horrors of war. While neither has dismissed the Just War tradition, they discuss war as though it is a horrible occurrence, which people of good will can avoid[cii]. Both pontiffs seem to accept an approach similar to the 'presumption against war'. Their reasoning and tone indicate that they understand war to be a terrible threat to humanity on a physical and spiritual level.

Pope John Paul II seemed to be more inclined to the idea of 'presumption against war' as he demonstrated in many of his public statements notably his messages for the World Day of Peace. Pope John Paul II was very strong in his language encouraging peace and discouraging war, while not emphasizing the need to clarify or further understand the Just War tradition. Pope John Paul II grew up in Poland during a time when the country was occupied by the Nazis followed by a communist occupation and he was no stranger to horrors of war or to reality of evil in the world[ciii]. He was not naïve. He understood that there were bad actors and mixed motives in the world. He stated in his message for the 1980 World Day of Peace, "The desire for peace does not cause a man of peace to shut his eyes to the tension, injustice and strife that are part of our world. He looks at them squarely."[civ] He believed that Jesus was the answer to the evil in the world and he did not believe war offered a positive solution to the problems facing humanity. In fact in an address to the Vatican Diplomatic Corps, January 13, 2003, Pope John Paul II stated, "War is not always inevitable. It is a defeat for humanity."[cv] As referred to earlier, he indicated, in his papal encyclical Centesimus Annus, that in a practical way non-violent means were part of the downfall of communism in eastern Europe, "Also worthy of emphasis is the fact that the fall of this kind of "bloc" or empire was accomplished almost everywhere by means of peaceful protest, using only the weapons of truth and justice."[cvi] This may have given him some sense of the real possibilities of a patient non-violent response to oppression and violence. Pope John Paul II had a realistic view of the world, but still he was inclined toward the 'presumption against war' view.

Pope John Paul II's view of the downfall of communism in Eastern Europe seemed to match his vision for a Christian response to violence in the world. He observed the suffering of people throughout Eastern Europe, living under oppressive Marxist regimes, who used coercion and violence to control their citizens. He experienced the oppression first-hand in Poland as a young man, a priest, and a bishop[cvii]. He also witnessed what he characterized as a mostly non-violent Christian response to the oppression. He eventually saw those oppressive regimes give out under the pressure of truth not force[cviii]. This seemed to express John Paul II's hope for the human response to evil in the world. Pope John Paul II's interpretation of the downfall of communism in Eastern Europe was a model for his idea of a Christian response to injustice in this world.

While this is true, Pope John Paul II promulgated the Catechism of the Catholic Church published in 1993, which contains the teachings regarding the Just War tradition, and one can assume if he did not approve of the tradition, he could have amended it or omitted it entirely. Pope John Paul II seemed not to emphasize the Just War tradition and from his remarks to the diplomatic corps it can be inferred that he had a 'presumption against war'. It is implied that he cherished peace so much and he understood peace to be the key path to a world in cooperation with God and that war, while it could be justified in certain circumstances, would never bear the fruit of justice at least not with the same impact of peace. War as a 'defeat for humanity' was a last resort in Pope John Paul II's mind and his statements imply that to focus too much on when it is permissible to conduct war is to look at faith and the world in a minimalist way. Pope John Paul II's statements regarding war and peace suggest a 'presumption against war' approach, but not an entirely pacifist position.

Pope Benedict XVI statements and writings also suggest a 'presumption against war' approach regarding war and he also did not make specific statements regarding the Just War tradition. Pope Benedict XVI was a little younger than Pope John Paul II, but he grew up in Germany during Nazism and similarly had been a witness to the depravity of some people and the depth to which humanity could sink. Similarly, Pope Benedict XVI decided he believed Jesus was the answer to the problems of the world, including violence.[cix] In his first message for the 2006 World Day of Peace, Pope Benedict XVI echoed many of the themes of Pope John Paul II and emphasized the need for true peace,

"Peace thus comes to be seen in a new light: not as the mere absence of war, but as a harmonious coexistence of individual citizens within a society governed by justice, one in which the good is also achieved, to the extent possible, for each of them."[cx]

He followed much of the logic of Pope John Paul II in his understanding that the real questions for Christians and for the world are more about how to achieve peace rather than appropriate times for war. However, in his message he does acknowledge tacitly a justification for war by discussing the necessity to conduct it with a sense of integrity, "The truth of peace must also let its beneficial light shine even amid the tragedy of war… 'not everything automatically becomes permissible between hostile parties once war has regrettably commenced'".[cxi] He even went so far as to discuss the virtue of military service and of military chaplaincy.[cxii] Pope Benedict XVI expressed admiration for "humanitarian law" and encouraged the idea of constantly seeking solutions other than war even when faced with terrorism. Pope Benedict XVI also appears to promote the notion of the 'presumption against war'.

Pope John Paul II and Pope Benedict XVI seem to maintain a 'presumption against war' and they are authoritative regarding Catholic teaching. They have expressed in their writings and statements a desire for justice and the promotion of the common good, but it seems they believe that war is so destructive, that often it disrupts justice irreparably. They promote justice, but they believe peace serves it better. Neither of the pontiffs are pacifist or even "functional pacifist"[cxiii] in their views. Their view is not that governments and the media are untrustworthy. They do acknowledge the need for proper authority and they do acknowledge the usefulness of the UN as a forum for those with grievances to have an opportunity to discuss their problems. They do express clearly that every effort for peace must be made and exhausted. Ultimately, the pontiffs seem to have a broader view of the world and the solutions for it. The view is not naïve, but war and finding justifications for war is not the priority. Peace is the priority. Pope John Paul II and Pope Benedict XVI seem to maintain a view of the Just War tradition that most closely resembles the 'presumption for peace', but it is more nuanced.

Questions and Suggestions

The discussion of the Catholic Just War tradition leads to questions, which are not resolved in this forum. One question involves the appropriate role of the UN and its appropriate understanding in relation to proper authority. This includes a discussion of the level of responsibility a specific leader of a nation has to the UN or the world community in questions of war and peace. The issue of whether it is justified in any circumstances for a nation to act unilaterally is another item, which could be examined further. These are some of the questions that arise for a discussion of the Catholic Just War tradition.

A discussion about the Catholic Just War tradition is useful, because it is a historical discussion as well as a philosophical one. It is useful to Catholics, because it enables them to reflect on the nature of war and how it interacts with their faith. That reflection enables them to better understand their own responsibilities as Catholics to be a witness of Jesus Christ. It is useful for non-Catholics, non-Christians, and atheists because it is useful to ask questions about right and wrong regarding war. Whether or not a person agrees with the Church, one can acknowledge that it is useful to look at the historical development of philosophical ideas regarding war and the human person in order to inform or give texture to one's own beliefs. The examination of the modern beliefs serves to further dissect the meaning of the teaching and better estimate its value. The use for a member of the US military is that it is important for warriors to understand justice so they better understand how to employ force under moral circumstances in a just manner.

While Pope Benedict understandably concerns himself with building the Kingdom of God through peaceful means, it would be useful for the Church to once again take up the question of the Just War tradition. It would be useful for the Church to study and debate the issue. It would be useful to bring Fr. John Dear, George Weigel, Dr Paul Griffiths, James Cardinal Stafford, other experts, and a chair from the Congregation for the Doctrine of the Faith for a series of seminars and discussion regarding the future of the Just War tradition. It would be important for the group to produce a report for the future pope's review. Upon review, the future pope could address the issue in a manner he sees fit, whether it be a papal letter, an encyclical, or in the message for the World Day of Peace. It would be useful for the faithful and for the world, despite their profound commitment to peace, to have clarification on the matter of the Just War tradition in the modern age.

Conclusion

The authoritative teaching on the Just War tradition from Pope John Paul II, Pope Benedict XVI, and the Catechism of the Catholic Church appears to acknowledge the three points of view discussed and falls between the notion of a 'presumption for peace' and the 'presumption for justice'. The pacifist view, discussed here includes ideas which the teachings of the Church support, but some ideas, which directly contradict the Catechism of the Catholic Church, such as the notion that serving in the military is immoral. George Weigel makes compelling arguments regarding the 'presumption for justice' but it appears the teachings of the Church, as voiced by the Catechism of the Catholic Church and upheld by statements of the Pope John Paul II and Pope Benedict XVI, have a 'both/and' approach. That approach is that Christians and the world in general should work for peace and peaceful solutions to all problems and that war should be a last resort after exhaustive and painstaking efforts to solve an issue peacefully. At the same time Christians must understand that peace is not an 'absence of war', but a condition of harmony and order in which human rights are respected and cultivated. Christians must never be satisfied with injustice, whether it is the repression of religious liberty, human trafficking, or economic injustice. Christians must work in peaceful, but forceful insistent ways to solve those problems in the world or peace will not exist. War is a tremendous threat to those things. There are circumstances and times when good people and legitimate nations or communities may have to conduct war, but only after every effort for peace has been exhausted. The Catholic Church teaching does have a 'presumption against war', but justice is an enduring ideal.

Endnotes

i Dear, John. *Put Down Your Sword: Answering the Call to Creative Nonviolence.(* Grand Rapids, MI: Wm. B. Eardmans Publishing Co, 2008.) 5

ii Griffiths, Paul J. "Just War: An Exchange." *First Things 122 (April 2002): 31-36.* http://georgeweigel.blogspot.com/

iii Griffiths, Paul J. "Just War: An Exchange." *First Things 122 (April 2002): 31-36.* http://georgeweigel.blogspot.com/

iv Dear, John. *Put Down Your Sword: Answering the Call to Creative Nonviolence. (*Grand Rapids, MI: Wm. B. Eardmans Publishing Co, 2008.) 5

v Griffiths, Paul J. "Just War: An Exchange." *First Things 122 (April 2002): 31-36.* http://georgeweigel.blogspot.com/

vi Weigel, George. "A peace that is Possible" *The Catholic Difference January 8, 2003.* http://georgeweigel.blogspot.com/

vii Pope John Paul II. *The Catechism of the Catholic Church.(* Libreria Editrice Vaticana, 1993). Part III, Section II, Chapter II, Article 5, Part III 2309 http://www.vatican.va/archive/ENG0015/ INDEX.HTM#fonte

viii *The Catechism of the Catholic Church.(* Libreria Editrice Vaticana, 1993). Part III, Section II, Chapter II, Article 5, Part I 2265 http://www.vatican.va/archive/ENG0015/ INDEX.HTM#fonte

ix *The Catechism of the Catholic Church.(* Libreria Editrice Vaticana, 1993). Part III, Section II, Chapter II, Article 5, Part III 2308 http://www.vatican.va/archive/ENG0015/ INDEX.HTM#fonte

x *The Catechism of the Catholic Church.(* Libreria Editrice Vaticana, 1993). Part III, Section II, Chapter II, Article 5, Part III 2308 http://www.vatican.va/archive/ENG0015/ INDEX.HTM#fonte

xi The Catechism of the Catholic Church.(Libreria Editrice Vaticana, 1993). Part III, Section II, Chapter II, Article 5, Part III 2309 http://www.vatican.va/archive/ENG0015/ INDEX.HTM#fonte

xii The Catechism of the Catholic Church.(Libreria Editrice Vaticana, 1993). Part III, Section II, Chapter II, Article 5, Part III 2310 http://www.vatican.va/archive/ENG0015/ INDEX.HTM#fonte

xiii New American Bible. (United States Conference of Catholic Bishops, 2013.) MK 12: 31 http://www.usccb.org/bible/books-of-the-bible/

xiv New American Bible. (United States Conference of Catholic Bishops, 2013.) MT 26: 52 http://www.usccb.org/bible/books-of-the-bible/

xv New American Bible. (United States Conference of Catholic Bishops, 2013.) MT 21:12-17 http://www.usccb.org/bible/books-of-the-bible/

xvi Weigel, George. *Tranquillitas Ordinis: The Present Failure and Future Promise of American Catholic Thought on War and Peace.(* New York, NY: Oxford University Press, 1987). 26

xvii New American Bible. (United States Conference of Catholic Bishops, 2013.) MK 12: 31 http://www.usccb.org/bible/books-of-the-bible/

xviii *The Catechism of the Catholic Church.(* Libreria Editrice Vaticana, 1993). Part III, Section II, Chapter II, Article 5, Part III 2310 http://www.vatican.va/archive/ENG0015/ INDEX.HTM#fonte

xix New American Bible. (United States Conference of Catholic Bishops, 2013.) MT 8:5-11 http://www.usccb.org/bible/books-of-the-bible/

xx New American Bible. (United States Conference of Catholic Bishops, 2013.) LK 3:14 http://www.usccb.org/bible/books-of-the-bible/

xxi Saint Augustine. *Contra Faustum: Book XXII, 77 (*New Advent, 2009.) 77 http://www.newadvent.org/fathers/140622.htm.

xxii Saint Augustine. *The City of God.* (Edited by Robert Maynard Hutchins Translated by Marcus Dods. Chicago, Il: Encyclopedia Britannica, Inc, 1952.) 515

xxiii Saint Augustine. *The City of God.* (Edited by Robert Maynard Hutchins Translated by Marcus Dods. Chicago, Il: Encyclopedia Britannica, Inc, 1952.) 515

xxiv Saint Augustine. (*The City of God.* Edited by Robert Maynard Hutchins Translated by Marcus Dods. Chicago, Il: Encyclopedia Britannica, Inc, 1952.)515

xxv Saint Augustine. *Contra Faustum: Book XXII, 77.* (New Advent, 2009.) 77 http://www.newadvent.org/fathers/140622.htm.

xxvi Saint Augustine. (*The City of God.* Edited by Robert Maynard Hutchins Translated by Marcus Dods. Chicago, Il: Encyclopedia Britannica, Inc, 1952.)515

xxvii Rhodes, Bill. *An Introduction to Military Ethics: A Reference Handbook.* (Santa Barbara, CA: ABC-CLIO,LLC, 2009.)26-27

xxviii Weigel, George. *Tranquillitas Ordinis: The Present Failure and Future Promise of American Catholic Thought on War and Peace.* (New York, NY: Oxford University Press, 1987). 27
Saint Augustine. *The City of God.* (Edited by Robert Maynard Hutchins Translated by Marcus Dods. Chicago, Il: Encyclopedia Britannica, Inc, 1952.) 323

xxix Rhodes, Bill. *An Introduction to Military Ethics: A Reference Handbook.* (Santa Barbara, CA: ABC-CLIO,LLC, 2009.)26-27

xxx Yoder, John Howard. *When War is Unjust: Being Honest in Just-War Thinking.* (Eugene, OR: Wipf and Stock Publishers, 1996.)17

xxxi Rhodes, Bill. *An Introduction to Military Ethics: A Reference Handbook.* (Santa Barbara, CA: ABC-CLIO,LLC, 2009.)27

xxxii Saint Thomas Aquinas. *Summa Theologica, Volume II.* (Edited by Robert Maynard Hutchins Translated by Fathers of the English Dominican Province. Chicago, Il: Encyclopedia Britannica, Inc, 1952.) 578

xxxiii Saint Thomas Aquinas. *Summa Theologica, Volume II.* (Edited by Robert Maynard Hutchins Translated by Fathers of the English Dominican Province. Chicago, Il: Encyclopedia Britannica, Inc, 1952.) 578

xxxiv Saint Thomas Aquinas. *Summa Theologica, Volume II.* (Edited by Robert Maynard Hutchins Translated by Fathers of the English Dominican Province. Chicago, Il: Encyclopedia Britannica, Inc, 1952.) 578

xxxv Weigel, George. *Tranquillitas Ordinis: The Present Failure and Future Promise of American Catholic Thought on War and Peace.* (New York, NY: Oxford University Press, 1987). 34, 35

xxxvi Weigel, George. *Tranquillitas Ordinis: The Present Failure and Future Promise of American Catholic Thought on War and Peace.* (New York, NY: Oxford University Press, 1987). 35, 36

xxxvii Weigel, George. *Tranquillitas Ordinis: The Present Failure and Future Promise of American Catholic Thought on War and Peace.* (New York, NY: Oxford University Press, 1987). 35

xxxviii Sheen, Fulton. "Conditions of a Just War" (*EWTN).* http://www.ewtn.com/library/ISSUES/SJUSTWAR.TXT

xxxix Weigel, George. *Tranquillitas Ordinis: The Present Failure and Future Promise of American Catholic Thought on War and Peace.* (New York, NY: Oxford University Press, 1987). 35, 36

xl Rhodes, Bill. *An Introduction to Military Ethics: A Reference Handbook.* (Santa Barbara, CA: ABC-CLIO,LLC, 2009.) 27

xli Weigel, George. *Tranquillitas Ordinis: The Present Failure and Future Promise of American Catholic Thought on War and Peace.* (New York, NY: Oxford University Press, 1987). 33

xlii Pope John Paul II. *The Catechism of the Catholic Church.* (Libreria Editrice Vaticana, 1993). Part III, Section II, Chapter II, Article 5, Part III 2308
http://www.vatican.va/archive/ENG0015/_INDEX.HTM#fonte

xliii Pope John Paul II. *The Catechism of the Catholic Church.* (Libreria Editrice Vaticana, 1993). Part III, Section II, Chapter II, Article 5, Part III 2309
http://www.vatican.va/archive/ENG0015/_INDEX.HTM#fonte

xliv Dear, John. "The Church After Pope John Paul II" *Fr John Dear 2001.* http://www.johndear.org/

xlv Dear, John. *Put Down Your Sword: Answering the Call to Creative Nonviolence.* (Grand Rapids, MI: Wm. B. Eardmans Publishing Co, 2008.) 4

xlvi Dear, John. *Put Down Your Sword: Answering the Call to Creative Nonviolence.* (Grand Rapids, MI: Wm. B. Eardmans Publishing Co, 2008.) 6

xlvii Day, Dorothy. "The Use of Force". *The Catholic Worker*, November 1936, 4. *The Catholic Worker Movement.* http://www.catholicworker.org/dorothyday/Reprint2.cfm?TextID=306.

xlviii Dear, John. "The Church After Pope John Paul II" *Fr John Dear 2001.*
http://www.johndear.org/

xlix Dear, John. "The Church After Pope John Paul II" *Fr John Dear 2001.*
http://www.johndear.org/

l Yoder, John Howard. *When War is Unjust: Being Honest in Just-War Thinking. (*Eugene, OR: Wipf and Stock Publishers, 1996.) 106

li Yoder, John Howard. *When War is Unjust: Being Honest in Just-War Thinking. (*Eugene, OR: Wipf and Stock Publishers, 1996.)106

lii Yoder, John Howard. *When War is Unjust: Being Honest in Just-War Thinking. (*Eugene, OR: Wipf and Stock Publishers, 1996.)106

liii Day, Dorothy. "The Use of Force". *The Catholic Worker*, November 1936, 4. *The Catholic Worker Movement.*
http://www.catholicworker.org/dorothyday/Reprint2.cfm?TextID=306.

liv Weigel, George. *Tranquillitas Ordinis: The Present Failure and Future Promise of American Catholic Thought on War and Peace.(*New York, NY: Oxford University Press, 1987). 30

lv Griffiths, Paul J. "Just War: An Exchange." *First Things 122 (April 2002): 31-36.*
http://georgeweigel.blogspot.com/

lvi Griffiths, Paul J. "Just War: An Exchange." *First Things 122 (April 2002): 31-36.*
http://georgeweigel.blogspot.com/

lvii Pope John Paul II. *The Catechism of the Catholic Church.(*Libreria Editrice Vaticana, 1993). Part III, Section II, Chapter II, Article 5, Part III 2308
http://www.vatican.va/archive/ENG0015/_INDEX.HTM#fonte

lviii Pope John Paul II. *The Catechism of the Catholic Church.(*Libreria Editrice Vaticana, 1993). Part III, Section II, Chapter II, Article 5, Part III. 2309
http://www.vatican.va/archive/ENG0015/_INDEX.HTM#fonte

lix Griffiths, Paul J. "Just War: An Exchange." *First Things 122 (April 2002): 31-36.*
http://georgeweigel.blogspot.com/

lx Griffiths, Paul J. "Just War: An Exchange." *First Things 122 (April 2002): 31-36.*
http://georgeweigel.blogspot.com/

lxi Weigel, George. *Tranquillitas Ordinis: The Present Failure and Future Promise of American Catholic Thought on War and Peace.(*New York, NY: Oxford University Press, 1987). 37

lxii Griffiths, Paul J. "Just War: An Exchange." *First Things 122 (April 2002): 31-36.*
http://georgeweigel.blogspot.com/

lxiii Griffiths, Paul J. "Just War: An Exchange." *First Things 122 (April 2002): 31-36.*
http://georgeweigel.blogspot.com/

lxiv Griffiths, Paul J. "Just War: An Exchange." *First Things 122 (April 2002): 31-36.*
http://georgeweigel.blogspot.com/

lxv Saint Thomas Aquinas. *Summa Theologica, Volume II.* (Edited by Robert Maynard Hutchins Translated by Fathers of the English Dominican Province. Chicago, Il: Encyclopedia Britannica, Inc, 1952.) 578

lxvi New American Bible. United States Conference of Catholic Bishops, 2013.
http://www.usccb.org/bible/books-of-the-bible/

lxvii Sheen, Fulton. "Conditions of a Just War" (*EWTN).*
http://www.ewtn.com/library/ISSUES/SJUSTWAR.TXT

lxviii *The Catechism of the Catholic Church.(*Libreria Editrice Vaticana, 1993). Part III, Section II, Chapter II, Article 5, Part III 2308

lxix Cardinal Stafford on War and the Church's Thinking, Zenit interview w. Cardinal Stafford. May 22, 2004.
http://georgeweigel.blogspot.com/

lxx Cardinal Stafford on War and the Church's Thinking, Zenit interview w. Cardinal Stafford. May 22, 2004.
http://georgeweigel.blogspot.com/

lxxi Russell Shaw on Iraq, Just War and Prudential Judgments, Zenit interview w. Russell Shaw. March 13, 2003.
http://www.zenit.org/en/articles/russell-shaw-on-iraq-just-war-and-prudential-judgments

lxxii Pope John Paul II. *The Catechism of the Catholic Church.(*Libreria Editrice Vaticana, 1993). Part III, Section II, Chapter II, Article 5, Part III 2308 lxxiii Pope John Paul II. *The Catechism of the Catholic Church.*(Libreria Editrice Vaticana, 1993). Part III, Section II, Chapter II, Article 5, Part III 2309

lxxiv Sheen, Fulton. "Conditions of a Just War" (*EWTN).*
http://www.ewtn.com/library/ISSUES/SJUSTWAR.TXT

lxxv Cardinal Stafford on War and the Church's Thinking, Zenit interview w. Cardinal Stafford. May 22, 2004.
http://georgeweigel.blogspot.com/

lxxvi Weigel, George. "A peace that is Possible" *The Catholic Difference January 8, 2003.*
http://georgeweigel.blogspot.com/

lxxvii Griffiths, Paul J. "Just War: An Exchange." *First Things 122 (April 2002): 31-36.*
http://georgeweigel.blogspot.com/

lxxviii Griffiths, Paul J. "Just War: An Exchange." *First Things 122 (April 2002): 31-36.*
http://georgeweigel.blogspot.com/

lxxix Griffiths, Paul J. "Just War: An Exchange." *First Things 122 (April 2002): 31-36.*
http://georgeweigel.blogspot.com/

lxxx Weigel, George. "A peace that is Possible" *The Catholic Difference January 8, 2003.*
http://georgeweigel.blogspot.com/

lxxxi Johnson, James Turner. "Just War: As It Was and Is." *First Things 149 (January 2005): 14-24.*
http://georgeweigel.blogspot.com/

lxxxii New American Bible. (United States Conference of Catholic Bishops, 2013.) MK 12: 31
http://www.usccb.org/bible/books-of-the-bible/

lxxxiii Pope John Paul II. *The Catechism of the Catholic Church.*(Libreria Editrice Vaticana, 1993). Part III, Section II, Chapter II, Article 5, Part I 2265

lxxxiv Weigel, George. "What is the Just War Tradition for?" *The Catholic Difference December 4, 2002.*
http://georgeweigel.blogspot.com/

lxxxv Weigel, George. "What is the Just War Tradition for?" *The Catholic Difference December 4, 2002.*
http://georgeweigel.blogspot.com/

lxxxvi Johnson, James Turner. "Just War: As It Was and Is." *First Things 149 (January 2005): 14-24.*
http://georgeweigel.blogspot.com/

lxxxvii Johnson, James Turner. "Just War: As It Was and Is." *First Things 149 (January 2005): 14-24.*
http://georgeweigel.blogspot.com/

lxxxviii Johnson, James Turner. "Just War: As It Was and Is." *First Things 149 (January 2005): 14-24.*
http://georgeweigel.blogspot.com/

lxxxix Pope John Paul II. *The Catechism of the Catholic Church.*(Libreria Editrice Vaticana, 1993). Part III, Section II, Chapter II, Article 5, Part III 2309
http://www.vatican.va/archive/ENG0015/_INDEX.HTM#fonte

xc Russell Shaw on Iraq, Just War and Prudential Judgments, Zenit interview w. Russell Shaw. March 13, 2003.

xci Weigel, George. "What is the Just War Tradition for?" *The Catholic Difference December 4, 2002.*
http://georgeweigel.blogspot.com/

xcii Griffiths, Paul J. "Just War: An Exchange." *First Things 122 (April 2002): 31-36.*
http://georgeweigel.blogspot.com/

xciii Griffiths, Paul J. "Just War: An Exchange." *First Things 122 (April 2002): 31-36.*
http://georgeweigel.blogspot.com/

xciv Johnson, James Turner. "Just War: As It Was and Is." *First Things 149 (January 2005): 14-24.*
http://georgeweigel.blogspot.com/

xcv Pope John Paul II. *The Catechism of the Catholic Church.*(Libreria Editrice Vaticana, 1993). Part III, Section II, Chapter II, Article 5, Part III 2313-2315
http://www.vatican.va/archive/ENG0015/_INDEX.HTM#fonte

xcvi Pope John Paul II. *The Catechism of the Catholic Church.*(Libreria Editrice Vaticana, 1993). Part III, Section II, Chapter II, Article 5, Part III 2313 -2315
http://www.vatican.va/archive/ENG0015/_INDEX.HTM#fonte

xcvii Griffiths, Paul J. "Just War: An Exchange." *First Things 122 (April 2002): 31-36.*
http://georgeweigel.blogspot.com/

xcviii Griffiths, Paul J. "Just War: An Exchange." *First Things 122 (April 2002): 31-36.*

http://georgeweigel.blogspot.com/
xcix Johnson, James Turner. "Just War: As It Was and Is." *First Things 149 (January 2005): 14-24.*
http://georgeweigel.blogspot.com/
c Pope Benedict XVI. Message. "InTruth Peace" *Message for the Celebration of the World Day of Peace* (2006 Comp.).
http://www.vatican.va/holy_father/benedict_xvi/messages/peace/index_en.htm
Pope John Paul II. Message. "Truth, The Power of Peace" *Message for the Celebration of the World Day of Peace* (1980 Comp.).
http://www.vatican.va/holy_father/john_paul_ii/messages/peace/index.htm
ci Pope Benedict XVI. Message. "InTruth Peace" *Message for the Celebration of the World Day of Peace* (2006 Comp.).
http://www.vatican.va/holy_father/benedict_xvi/messages/peace/index_en.htm
Pope John Paul II. Message. "Truth, The Power of Peace" *Message for the Celebration of the World Day of Peace* (1980 Comp.).
http://www.vatican.va/holy_father/john_paul_ii/messages/peace/index.htm
cii Pope John Paul II. "Address of His Holiness Pope John Paul II to the Diplomatice Corps." Speech to the Vatican Diplomatic Corps Libreria Editrice Vaticana, January 2003. 4
http://www.vatican.va/holy_father/john_paul_ii/speeches/2003/january/documents/hf_jp-ii_spe_20030113_diplomatic-corps_en.html
ciii Weigel, George. *Witness to Hope: The Biography of Pope John Paul II.(* New York, NY: Harper Collins Publishers, 2005.) Ch 2
civ Pope John Paul II. Message. "Truth, The Power of Peace" *Message for the Celebration of the World Day of Peace* (1980 Comp.). 5
http://www.vatican.va/holy_father/john_paul_ii/messages/peace/index.htm
cv Pope John Paul II. "Address of His Holiness Pope John Paul II to the Diplomatice Corps." Speech to the Vatican Diplomatic Corps Libreria Editrice Vaticana, January 2003. 4
http://www.vatican.va/holy_father/john_paul_ii/speeches/2003/january/documents/hf_jp-ii_spe_20030113_diplomatic-corps_en.html
cvi Pope John Paul II. *Centesimus Annus. (*Libreria Editrice Vaticana, 1991.) 23
http://www.vatican.va/holy_father/john_paul_ii/encyclicals/documents/hf_jp-ii_enc_01051991_centesimus-annus_en.html
cvii Weigel, George. *Witness to Hope: The Biography of Pope John Paul II.(* New York, NY: Harper Collins Publishers, 2005.) Ch 2
cviii Pope John Paul II. *Centesimus Annus. (*Libreria Editrice Vaticana, 1991.) 23
http://www.vatican.va/holy_father/john_paul_ii/encyclicals/documents/hf_jp-ii_enc_01051991_centesimus-annus_en.html
cix Weigel, George. "A New Pope Must Face Old Problems" *Los Angeles Times* December 30, 2005.
http://georgeweigel.blogspot.com/
cx Pope Benedict XVI. Message. "InTruth Peace" *Message for the Celebration of the World Day of Peace* (2006 Comp.). 6
http://www.vatican.va/holy_father/benedict_xvi/messages/peace/index_en.htm
cxi Pope Benedict XVI. Message. "InTruth Peace" *Message for the Celebration of the World Day of Peace* (2006 Comp.). 7
http://www.vatican.va/holy_father/benedict_xvi/messages/peace/index_en.htm
cxii Pope Benedict XVI. Message. "InTruth Peace" *Message for the Celebration of the World Day of Peace* (2006 Comp.). 8
http://www.vatican.va/holy_father/benedict_xvi/messages/peace/index_en.htm
cxiii Griffiths, Paul J. "Just War: An Exchange." *First Things 122 (April 2002): 31-36.*
http://georgeweigel.blogspot.com/

Bibliography

Dear, John. *Put Down Your Sword: Answering the Call to Creative Nonviolence.* Grand Rapids, MI: Wm. B. Eardmans Publishing Co, 2008.

Yoder, John Howard. *When War is Unjust: Being Honest in Just-War Thinking.* Eugene, OR: Wipf and Stock Publishers, 1996.

Rhodes, Bill. *An Introduction to Military Ethics: A Reference Handbook.* Santa Barbara, CA: ABC-CLIO,LLC, 2009.

Weigel, George. *Tranquillitas Ordinis: The Present Failure and Future Promise of American Catholic Thought on War and Peace.* New York, NY: Oxford University Press, 1987.

Weigel, George. *God's Choice: Pope Benedict XVI and the Future of the Catholic Church.* New York, NY: Harper Collins Publishers, 1999.

Weigel, George. *Witness to Hope: The Biography of Pope John Paul II.* New York, NY: Harper Collins Publishers, 2005.

Pope John Paul II. *The Catechism of the Catholic Church.* Libreria Editrice Vaticana, 1993. http://www.vatican.va/archive/ENG0015/_INDEX.HTM#fonte

Saint Augustine. *The City of God.* Edited by Robert Maynard Hutchins Translated by Marcus Dods. Chicago, Il: Encyclopedia Britannica, Inc, 1952.

Saint Augustine. *Contra Faustum: Book XXII, 77.* New Advent, 2009. http://www.newadvent.org/fathers/140622.htm.

Saint Thomas Aquinas. *Summa Theologica, Volume II.* Edited by Robert Maynard Hutchins Translated by Fathers of the English Dominican Province. Chicago, Il: Encyclopedia Britannica, Inc, 1952.

New American Bible. United States Conference of Catholic Bishops, 2013. http://www.usccb.org/bible/books-of-the-bible/

Griffiths, Paul J. "Just War: An Exchange." *First Things 122 (April 2002): 31-36.* http://georgeweigel.blogspot.com/

Cardinal Stafford on War and the Church's Thinking, Zenit interview w. Cardinal Stafford. May 22, 2004. http://georgeweigel.blogspot.com/

Weigel, George. "Reality of terrorism calls for a fresh look at the Just War Tradition." *The Catholic Difference Sept. 20, 2001.*

http://georgeweigel.blogspot.com/

Weigel, George. "Just War and Pre-emption: Three Questions." *The Catholic Difference October 2, 2002.*
http://georgeweigel.blogspot.com/

Weigel, George. "A peace that is Possible" *The Catholic Difference January 8, 2003.*
http://georgeweigel.blogspot.com/

Weigel, George. "What is the Just War Tradition for?" *The Catholic Difference December 4, 2002.*
http://georgeweigel.blogspot.com/

Weigel, George. "A New Pope Must Face Old Problems" *Los Angeles Times* December 30, 2005.
http://georgeweigel.blogspot.com/

Dear, John. "The Church After Pope John Paul II" *Fr John Dear 2001.*
http://www.johndear.org/

Dear, John. *"The Eucharist and Nonviolence: Remembering, Reconciling, and Sending Us Forth to Make Peace" Fr John Dear April 5, 2004.*
http://www.johndear.org/

Pope Benedict XVI. Message. "InTruth Peace" *Message for the Celebration of the World Day of Peace* (2006 Comp.).
http://www.vatican.va/holy_father/benedict_xvi/messages/peace/index_en.htm

Pope John Paul II. Message. "To Reach Peace, Teach Peace" *Message for the Celebration of the World Day of Peace* (1979 Comp.).
http://www.vatican.va/holy_father/john_paul_ii/messages/peace/index.htm

Pope John Paul II. Message. "Truth, The Power of Peace" *Message for the Celebration of the World Day of Peace* (1980 Comp.).
http://www.vatican.va/holy_father/john_paul_ii/messages/peace/index.htm

Pope John Paul II. Message. "From Justice of Each comes Peace for All" *Message for the Celebration of the World Day of Peace* (1998 Comp.).
http://www.vatican.va/holy_father/john_paul_ii/messages/peace/index.htm

Pope John Paul II. Message. "Respect for Human Rights: The Secret of True Peace" *Message for the Celebration of the World Day of Peace* (1999 Comp.).
http://www.vatican.va/holy_father/john_paul_ii/messages/peace/index.htm

Pope John Paul II. Message. "To Reach Peace, Teach Peace" *Message for the Celebration of the World Day of Peace* (1979 Comp.).
http://www.vatican.va/holy_father/john_paul_ii/messages/peace/index.htm

Pope John Paul II. "Address of His Holiness Pope John Paul II to the Diplomatice Corps." Speech to the Vatican Diplomatic Corps   Libreria Editrice Vaticana, January 2003.
http://www.vatican.va/holy_father/john_paul_ii/speeches/2003/january/documents/hf_jp-ii_spe_20030113_diplomatic-corps_en.html

Pope John Paul II. *Centesimus Annus*. Libreria Editrice Vaticana, 1991.
http://www.vatican.va/holy_father/john_paul_ii/encyclicals/documents/hf_jp-ii_enc_01051991_centesimus-annus_en.html

Pope John XXIII. *Pacem in Terris*. Libreria Editrice Vaticana, 1963.
http://www.vatican.va/holy_father/john_xxiii/encyclicals/documents/hf_j-xxiii_enc_11041963_pacem_en.html

Sheen, Fulton. "Conditions of a Just War" *EWTN*.
http://www.ewtn.com/library/ISSUES/SJUSTWAR.TXT

Shaw, Russell. "The Iraq Debate: The War Was Unjust" Crisis Magazine 2007
http://crisismagazine.com/2007/the-iraq-debate-the-war-was-unjust

Russell Shaw on Iraq, Just War and Prudential Judgments, Zenit interview w. Russell Shaw. March 13, 2003.
http://www.zenit.org/en/articles/russell-shaw-on-iraq-just-war-and-prudential-judgments

Johnson, James Turner. "Just War: As It Was and Is." *First Things 149 (January 2005): 14-24.*
http://georgeweigel.blogspot.com/

Day, Dorothy. "The Use of Force". *The Catholic Worker*, November 1936, 4. *The Catholic Worker Movement*. http://www.catholicworker.org/dorothyday/Reprint2.cfm?TextID=306.

www.ingramcontent.com/pod-product-compliance
Lightning Source LLC
Chambersburg PA
CBHW080616290526
45790CB00007B/2803